Naming Words

Nouns and Pronouns

Anita Ganeri

Heinemann Library
Chicago, Illinois

www.capstonepub.com
Visit our website to find out more information about Heinemann-Raintree books.

To order:
☎ Phone 888-454-2279
🖥 Visit www.capstonepub.com to browse our catalog and order online.

© 2012 Heinemann Library
an imprint of Capstone Global Library, LLC
Chicago, Illinois

Edited by Daniel Nunn, Rebecca Rissman, and Sian Smith
Designed by Joanna Hinton-Malivoire
Picture research by Tracy Cummins
Original illustrations © Capstone Global Library
Illustrated by Joanna Hinton-Malivoire
Production by Eirian Griffiths
Originated by Capstone Global Library Ltd
Printed and bound in China by South China Printing Company Ltd

15 14 13 12 11
10 9 8 7 6 5 4 3 2 1

Library of Congress Cataloging-in-Publication Data
Ganeri, Anita, 1961-
  Naming words : nouns and pronouns / Anita Ganeri.
    p. cm.—(Getting to grips with grammar)
  Includes bibliographical references and index.
  ISBN 978-1-4329-5806-0 (hbk) ISBN 978-1-4329-5813-8 (pbk)
  1. English language—Noun—Juvenile literature. 2. English language—Pronoun—Juvenile literature. 3. English language—Grammar—Juvenile literature. I. Title.
  PE1205.G36 2012
  428.1—dc22
                            2011014702

Acknowledgments
We would like to thank the following for permission to reproduce photographs and artworks: Dreamstime.com pp.22 (© Fotomorgana), 26 (© Annminina); istockphoto p.24 (© Linda Kloosterhof); Shutterstock pp.5 (© Greg da Silva), 6 (© Bannykh Alexey Vladimirovich), 7 (© Dmitry Naumov), 8 left (© M. Unal Ozmen), 8 right (© joingate), 9 (© p.schwarz), 10 (© Iwona Grodzka), 11 (© Kletr), 13 (© Vaclav Volrab), 14 (© JungleOutThere), 15 (© Gorelova), 17 (© joingate), 18 (© Viorel Sima), 19 (© Monkey Business Images), 20 (© Studio 1One), 25 (© Big Pants Production), 27 (© Cory Thoman), 28 (© i359702), 30 (© AJP).

Every effort has been made to contact copyright holders of any material reproduced in this book. Any omissions will be rectified in subsequent printings if notice is given to the publisher.

Contents

Some words are shown in bold, **like this**
You can find them in the glossary on page 31.

What Is Grammar?

Grammar is a set of rules that helps you to write and speak a language. Grammar is important because it helps people to understand each other.

went Today swimming. I in the ocean

Without grammar, this **sentence** doesn"t make sense.

In grammar, words are divided into different types. These are called parts of speech. They show how words are used. This book is about parts of speech called **nouns**.

Today I went swimming in the ocean.

Grammar turns the jumbled-up words into a sentence.

What Is a Noun?

A **noun** is a naming word. A noun is used to name a person, an animal, a place, or a thing.

The dog barked at the cat.

"Dog" and "cat" are nouns. They tell you the names of the animals.

The **boy** is riding a **bike**.

"Boy" and "bike" are nouns. They tell you the names of someone and something.

It is easy to find out if something is a noun. If a word tells you the name of someone or something, it is a noun.

Spot the Noun

Look at this list of words. Can you pick out all the **nouns** in the list? Remember that a noun is a naming word.

sandy

bucket

spade

ice cream

quickly

sandcastle

"Bucket," "spade," "ice cream," and "sandcastle" are nouns. "Sandy" and "quickly" are *not* nouns.

Look at the three **sentences** below. How many nouns can you spot? There is one noun in the first sentence, two in the second sentence, and three in the third.

The nouns are "lion," "bird," "sky," "flowers," "trees," and "yard."

The lion is roaring.

A bird flies in the sky.

Flowers and trees grow in the yard.

"The," "a," and "an"

Nouns often have "the," "a," or "an" in front of them. Try putting "the" in front of the words in this list. Which words are *not* nouns?

bird

tree

flower

kite

sometimes

pretty

"Sometimes" and "pretty" are not nouns. You can't say "the sometimes" or "the pretty."

"Antelope" begins with a vowel. "Giraffe" begins with a consonant.

An antelope can run very fast.

A giraffe is very tall.

We use "an" if a noun begins with a **vowel**. The vowels are "a," "e," "i," "o," and "u." We use "a" if a noun begins with a **consonant.** A consonant is any of the other letters.

Singular or Plural?

Nouns can be **singular** or **plural**.
A singular noun names one person or thing. You can put "a" or "an" in front of it.

"Sister" and "brother" are both singular nouns.

I have a sister and a brother.

Plural nouns name two or more people or things. You usually make plurals by adding "s" to the end of a word.

Dinosaurs were enormous creatures.

"Dinosaurs" and "creatures" are plural nouns. The singular for these words are "dinosaur" and "creature."

Common Nouns

A common **noun** is a noun that names a type of person or thing. Common nouns can be **singular** or **plural**.

The words in the list are all common nouns.

windows

building

shops

town

street

I like reading **books**.

Some people **look very old.**

"Books" and "people" are common nouns.

Common nouns are used to name general people or things. They are not used to name particular people or things.

Proper Nouns

A proper **noun** is the name of a particular person, place, or thing. Proper nouns always begin with a **capital letter**.

Wednesday

New York

David

Market Street

Spain

The nouns in this list are all proper nouns.

Proper nouns usually name things that are one of a kind. You can't put "the," "a," or "an" in front of many proper nouns.

I was born in March.

"March" is a proper noun. It is the name of a particular month.

Collective Nouns

A collective **noun** is a noun that describes a group. This can be a group of people, animals, or things.

a herd of cows

a bunch of flowers

In these examples "herd" and "bunch" are collective nouns.

In the lists below there are four collective nouns and four groups. Can you match the collective nouns to their groups?

flock	**soccer players**
swarm	**sheep**
team	**playing cards**
pack	**bees**

The answers are:
a flock of sheep,
a swarm of bees,
a team of soccer players,
a pack of playing cards.

Abstract Nouns

Abstract **nouns** are used to describe feelings or qualities. These are things that you cannot see, hear, touch, taste, or smell.

"Happiness" is an abstract noun.

She was filled with happiness.

beauty

sadness

honesty

love

fear

Abstract nouns do not usually have **plurals**.

Look at the list above. All of the nouns in the list are abstract nouns. Can you think of any more?

More Plurals

Some **plural nouns** are formed in different ways. If a word ends in "ss," "sh," "ch," or "x," you need to add "es."

The **foxes** came into the yard.

"Foxes" is plural. The **singular** is "fox."

For words that end in "y," you take away the "y" and change the ending to "ies." But if there is a **vowel** before the "y," just add "s." Some plurals, such as "children" or "sheep," don't follow rules. You just have to learn them.

In summer, there are lots of flies.

The children are playing outside.

Sheep eat grass.

"Flies" is plural. The singular is "fly."
"Children" is plural. The singular is "child."
"Sheep" can be both singular and plural!

What Is a Pronoun?

A **pronoun** is a word that is used to stand for a **noun**. You use a pronoun so that you do not have to use the same noun over and over again.

Anna **strokes the cat.** She **loves it.**

"She" is a pronoun. It stands for "Anna." "It" is a pronoun. It stands for "the cat."

The children **washed** their hands. **Then** they **dried** them.

"They" is a plural pronoun. It stands for "the children." "Them" is a plural pronoun. It stands for "their hands."

Pronouns can be **singular** or **plural**. In a **sentence**, they stand for singular or plural nouns.

Personal Pronouns

A personal **pronoun** stands for a person. It can be the **subject** of a **sentence**. This means it is the person doing the action.

The queen sat on the throne.

or

She sat on the throne.

"She" is a personal pronoun. It stands for "the queen." It is the subject of the sentence.

A personal pronoun can also be the **object** of a sentence. This means it is the person the action is being done to. An action or a doing word is called a **verb**.

"Him" stands for "Josh." It is the object of the sentence.

The bear chased Josh.
or
The bear chased him.

Possessive Pronouns

Some **pronouns** are used to show that something belongs to someone. They are called **possessive** pronouns.

"Mine" is a possessive pronoun. It stands for "my house."

Becky's house is bigger than mine.

This is my hat. Why don't you wear yours?

In this sentence "yours" is a possessive pronoun. It stands for "your hat."

The words "mine," "yours," "ours," "theirs," "his," and "hers" are possessive pronouns. Each one can stand in place of a noun. They show who things belong to.

Find the Nouns

How many **nouns** can you think of that fit with the picture below?

Possible answers: elephant, elephants, man, men, woman, women, umbrella, umbrellas, dresses, decorations, sticks, shirts, clothes

Glossary

capital letter an upper-case letter, such as B, F, or Z

consonant a letter that is not a, e, i, o, or u

grammar a set of rules that helps you speak or write clearly

noun a naming word

object the person or thing a verb is being done to

plural meaning more than one person or thing

possessive meaning that something belongs to someone

pronoun a word that stands for a noun

sentence a group of words that makes sense on its own

singular meaning one person or one thing

subject the person or thing that is doing a verb

verb a doing or action word

vowel the letter a, e, i, o, or u

Find Out More

Books

Cleary, Brian A. *A Cat, a Bat, Your Grandma's Hat: What Is a Noun?*
Minneapolis, MN: Lerner Books, 2010.

Dahl, Michael. *If You Were a Noun.* Mankato, MN: Picture Window Books,
2007.

Websites

http://www.funbrain.com/grammar/
This fun Website asks readers to spot the parts of speech in different
sentences.

http://www.abcya.com/noun_verb_game/nouns_and_verbs.htm
Use this fun Website to practice identifying nouns and verbs.

Index